Original title:

The Pothos Promise

Copyright © 2025 Creative Arts Management OÜ
All rights reserved.

Author: Alec Donovan
ISBN HARDBACK: 978-1-80581-932-5
ISBN PAPERBACK: 978-1-80581-459-7
ISBN EBOOK: 978-1-80581-932-5

Whispers of Verdant Life

In the corner, green vines sway,
Chasing sunlight, come what may.
They stretch and reach, a friendly race,
Bringing smiles, all over the place.

Tangled laughter fills the room,
As leaves decide to take up bloom.
They whisper secrets, soft and sly,
While I just sit and wonder why.

A twist, a turn, what's this they do?
Climbing up, they've formed a crew.
With every inch, they laugh aloud,
Befriending all, they draw a crowd.

Branching Out into Tomorrow

With every leaf a new charade,
They prance and twirl, a lively parade.
Roots of joy in soil so deep,
While nearby, my worries sleep.

Dreaming big, they reach for stars,
Tipping pots and filling jars.
Each tendril whispers, 'We can fly!'
I can't help but laugh and sigh.

Branches twist in funny ways,
Creating stories for our days.
Tomorrow's plans with a dancey spin,
As I join in, let the fun begin.

Nurtured Connections

In the sunlight, they like to chat,
I catch them giggling, imagine that!
A leaf winks over at the fern,
'Did you see how fast the sun can burn?'

Pot friends whisper, sharing tales,
Of garden gnomes and wind-swept sails.
They bond like glue in this bright place,
In leafy laughter, they embrace grace.

With each sprout, a new story blooms,
Inviting joy to fill the rooms.
Their little winks and cheeky grins,
Make the mundane feel like wins.

Climbers in the City

In a concrete jungle, they aspire,
Climbing high, they never tire.
Two vines tango, side by side,
Chasing clouds, with endless pride.

They wrap around a lamp post bold,
Exchanging secrets, gossip untold.
'Hey, did you see the pigeon fly?'
Cackling leaves, oh my, oh my!

Through windowpanes, they tease the light,
Their leafy antics a pure delight.
With every twist, they conquer fears,
Bringing laughter through the years.

Roots Beneath the Surface

In the soil where secrets lie,
Worms and roots throw a wild party.
The pothos whispers, 'Don't be shy!'
While frisky leaves dance all hearty.

Dig a little deeper, friend,
To find the jokes that nature sends.
With every twist, a plot to bend,
Life's tangled fun never ends.

Golden Hues of Healing

A sprinkle of sun and a dash of rain,
Leaves laugh softly, forgetting pain.
With golden hues, they share the gain,
A plant with jokes — it's quite insane!

Healing vibes in every leaf,
Gather 'round for nature's brief.
Make a wish or share a grief,
Pothos humor, oh so chief.

Echoes of Growth

Giggles echo when roots expand,
Whispering tales of a green band.
Upward, they reach, hand in hand,
In the wild forest, totally unplanned.

With each new shoot, the puns take flight,
As the vines stretch out, what a sight!
Morning munchies, leaves take a bite,
In this green world, everything's light.

Nature's Silent Pact

In quiet corners where shadows play,
Plants conspire in a leafy way.
Nonsense erupts, come what may,
As vines giggle through the day.

They signed a pact without a sound,
To spread joy in the underground.
Take a seat and gather 'round,
For nature's jokes can astound!

Roots of Desire

In the corner, green and sly,
A little plant winks at passersby.
Its roots spread wide, a secret tale,
Whispering dreams of the next leafy trail.

Sipping coffee, oh what a tease,
This pot of joy can't help but please.
It wiggles its leaves with a sly little cheer,
As if saying, 'Stay close, my dear!'

The Unfurling Path

With every dawn, it stretches wide,
Leaves unfurling in their leafy pride.
Like a dancer on a sunlit stage,
Twisting and turning, setting the rage.

A leaf here, a vine there, grows anew,
Craving sunlight, but watering too.
It guffaws as it reaches out,
In its leafy kingdom, there's no doubt.

Flourish in the Quiet

In stillness lies a secret spree,
Where leaves sip whispers, carefree and free.
They giggle softly, bask in the light,
Plotting mischief till out of sight.

Oh, what joy in a humble home,
From corner shadows, they tend to roam.
Plant friends laughing in a cozy den,
Sowing wild tales again and again.

Green Enchantment

In the midst of pots and soil galore,
A twist of fate brings laughter to the floor.
With every leaf, a prank unfolds,
Stories of mischief in whispers retold.

When visitors talk, it eavesdrops keen,
Nods of approval, full of green sheen.
It grows and giggles in leafy delight,
A playful spirit, shining so bright.

Shadows of Promise

In the corner, leaves do creep,
Dreaming of secrets, not too deep.
They chuckle and wiggle with delight,
Chasing shadows in the moonlight.

A little water, a bit of sun,
They giggle as they sneak and run.
Roots are tangled in a race,
In this playful, leafy space.

With every droplet, a tale unfolds,
Of clumsy plants and their bold holds.
They whisper softly, 'Watch us grow!'
With each new leaf, they steal the show.

So raise a glass to growing green,
In every pot, a silly scene.
For leafy friends with humor bright,
Bring joy and laughter to our sight.

Reaching for the Light

Up towards the window, they all bend,
Stretching and swaying, what a blend!
With little vines that twist and twirl,
Reaching for light, giving a whirl.

They argue over who gets the sun,
In this leafy battle, there's no fun.
With petals puffed and whispers loud,
They giggle softly, oh so proud.

A little twist, a silly dance,
In sunlight's warmth, they love to prance.
Each leaf wants to be the star,
In this bright show, they all go far.

So let them climb and let them gleam,
In this wild and wondrous dream.
For in the chase for rays so bright,
They find their joy, day and night.

Nurtured by Stillness

In the quiet room, they find their peace,
Sipping the still air, life won't cease.
With dusty shelves as their backdrop,
They laugh and grow, no need to stop.

Pots all nestled, snug and tight,
Whispering secrets in the night.
A gentle breeze, a rustle here,
Brings giggles soft that we can hear.

From dirt to bloom, they take their time,
In perfect rhythm, like a rhyme.
With patience grand, they spread their cheer,
Bringing humor close and ever near.

So let them thrive in tranquil space,
For every plant's a smiling face.
In stillness, life blooms, oh so rare,
Join in the fun, if you dare!

Embracing the Unknown

In every twist, there's humor hid,
As little greens go where they bid.
With tangled roots and curious vines,
They venture forth, crossing all lines.

Each pot a treasure, what's inside?
With leaves that giggle, they take pride.
They bounce and bounce with every shake,
In the unknown, joy they make.

The world beyond, so vast and wide,
They tread with glee on this wild ride.
With every challenge, they hash it out,
For the thrill of growth, they dance and shout.

So let us join their leafy fun,
As they embrace each leap or run.
In life's great garden, come what may,
A little humor lights the way.

Petals in the Past

In a garden of memory, we twirl,
Where petals once danced, and leaves would swirl.
I tripped on a vine, fell flat on my face,
The flowers just laughed, at my clumsy grace.

A butterfly giggled, said 'What a sight!'
I brushed off the soil, embracing the light.
With petals in hand, I strutted like a king,
Claiming my throne in the chaos of spring.

A Journey Upward

Climbing a trellis, I reach for the sun,
Each leaf whispers secrets of joy and fun.
My cat's on a mission to chase every bug,
As I dangle below, feeling quite snug.

With vines wrapping round like a game of charades,
I climb with a grin, dodging garden blades.
The roses all chuckle as I slip and sway,
In this playful ascent, I find my own way.

The Silent Guardian

A cactus stands watch with a prickly grin,
While vines schemed to steal the sun's golden spin.
No need for guards in this garden so bright,
They sip on the dew, and plot late at night.

Mice in the shadows play poker 'til dawn,
While daisies debate if their petals are drawn.
The guardian smiles, with thorns like a crown,
In a world full of giggles, he never frowns down.

Memories on a Vine

In tangled up laughter, we climb the old wall,
Each leaf holds a story, a giggle, a fall.
I found an old shoe, the vine wrapped around,
A memory of adventures, where fun knows no bound.

With toddlers and snails, we dance hand in hand,
In this quirky green kingdom, a bizarre band.
Each twist and each turn, a tickle, a tease,
In the laughter of vines, my heart finds its ease.

Refreshing the Soul

A plant in the pot, so full of cheer,
It waves at the sun, as if to say, "Hey, dear!"
With leaves like confetti in a sunny parade,
It stretches and yawns, never ready to fade.

It dances with dust in a charming ballet,
Whispering secrets in its own leafy way.
When water arrives, it sips with glee,
"Oh, life's such a party! Come join me, you'll see!"

Renewal of Connection

A vine gives a wink, the gardener grins,
In this green little world, friendship begins.
Tendrils entwined like awkward first dates,
They giggle and twist, oh, the fun that awaits!

Together they thrive, a quirky duo,
Taking over the room, putting on quite a show.
When friends meet new leaves, the joy never ends,
In the heart of the home, where laughter transcends.

Librarian of the Leaf

With leaves like pages, it tells tales of sun,
A librarian of life, oh what fun!
Each curl and each twist, an adventure to see,
In chlorophyll chapters, it's wild and free.

It shushes the silence, with rustling delight,
As the breeze turns the pages, it's purely a sight.
Whispering wisdom from roots to the sky,
The stories of laughter, oh my, oh my!

Love Leaves a Mark

In the corner it stands, a confidant bright,
With stories of love that danced in the light.
A witness to secrets, both silly and sweet,
Its heart-shaped leaves bring us joy in retreat.

With every new leaf, a memory made,
In its leafy embrace, all worries do fade.
For love's just a plant that grows by your side,
A humorous journey on this wild ride!

Verdant Vows

I swore to water my leafy friend,
Hoping it's not just a trend.
But all it wants is a sunny spot,
And maybe a sip, just a tiny lot!

My green companion starts to grin,
With every leaf, I feel the win.
Yet when I trip, right on its vine,
Who knew plants had a sense of design!

I whisper secrets, soft and low,
In exchange, it grows, puts on a show.
With every promise made, we'll survive,
Even if its growth leaves me high-strive!

A vine that laughs, a plant that plays,
In this abode of sunlit rays.
Together we'll climb, with style and flair,
Witnessing moments without a care.

Unfurling Secrets

When leaves unravel, secrets arise,
In my green house, laughter complies.
The plant giggles when I'm not around,
Pretending I'm grand, while it's plants abound!

I reach to prune, but it leaps away,
Like a game of tag, oh what a display!
As I chase the stems, they shimmy and dance,
I swear they're mocking my garden romance!

Every twist and turn is full of cheer,
A funky routine, my plant's premiere.
I swear it grows just to make me swoon,
This playful plant, beneath the moon!

Through potted plots and sunny seams,
We chase our dreams in leafy beams.
With every turn, it teases my fate,
Who knew gardening could be this great?

Secret Gardens Within

In a hidden nook, where plants collide,
Secrets flourish, where blooms abide.
A garden giggles, behind the fence,
Crafting mischief, making no sense!

With petals swaying, in a warm embrace,
My leafy friends are on a race.
One hops left, another one spins,
Who knew they'd all declare their wins?

I sneak a peek, they're plotting schemes,
Watering cans turn into dreams.
In this whimsical botanical play,
Laughter blooms like flowers in May!

As vines entangle in curious twirls,
The garden whispers and softly swirls.
Every day's a fun surprise to find,
Nature's jesters, ever so kind!

Life's Climbing Companions

With every twist, my plants ascend,
Together we cherish, around each bend.
They giggle as they reach for the sky,
In our leafy realm, we'll never say bye!

They dangle down with clever flair,
A competition in mid-air dare.
Who says that climbing's just for trees?
Watch the hilarity, just see the ease!

Their tendrils wrap around my fate,
Encouragement shoots, I can't be late.
Together we rise, we glide, we sway,
In this green journey, come what may!

Through laughter and greens, we climb and zest,
In this plant-filled life, we know we're blessed.
With each leaf unfurled, a new story spins,
My rowdy companions, delight always wins!

Echoes in the Green

In the jungle of my room, it sprawls,
A daring vine that climbs the walls.
Whispers of green, a leafy tease,
It laughs at me, oh, with such ease.

I water it, but where's the root?
It dances high in search of fruit.
But all it does is grow and sway,
While I just hope it'll save the day.

With each new leaf, it drapes its charm,
Telling tales without a qualm.
In this green kingdom, I'm just a pawn,
While my leafy friend keeps moving on.

Invisible hands that pull and stretch,
In this comedy, who will fetch?
For every flower that holds a laugh,
There's a potbound joke on our green gaffe.

Spiral of Existence

In a pot of dreams, I find my muse,
A twisty vine in bright green shoes.
It spirals high with flair and glee,
Mocking me, oh, can't you see?

As I water, it says, 'Just wait!'
I roll my eyes, is this fate?
For every curl I chase and wish,
It finds new heights — that sneaky fish!

Its leaves are like a magic spell,
Growing wild and hard to quell.
But as it climbs on every chair,
I keep on laughing, unaware.

In this spiral, who's the boss?
The vine, or me? Oh, what a toss!
With each odd turn, a giggle explodes,
As my plant's antics compile in codes.

Green Threads of Life

Among the green, a tale unfolds,
With threads of laughter, I've been told.
Each leaf a quirk upon a thread,
Ensuring joy in every spread.

It dangles down, a playful tease,
Frolicking free, it aims to please.
Human hearts, it brings delight,
Wrapping around with sheer insight.

Plotting schemes behind my back,
It stretches wide, 'This is our track.'
With every twist, it pulls at fate,
Pulling me in — oh, isn't it great?

So here we are, a duo surreal,
A plant so witty with endless appeal.
In the tapestry of life so bright,
We weave our tales both day and night.

A Vine's Voyage

A lonesome vine with dreams so grand,
Setting sail in a tiny land.
With twists and turns, it finds its way,
Chasing the sun, come what may.

Across the shelf, it scans the room,
With little hops, it seeks to bloom.
Each new leaf a hopeful shout,
'Adventure calls, no time for doubt!'

Oh, the stories it has to tell,
Of daring climbs and tumbles that fell.
In this wild voyage, who could foresee,
The laughter stirred in its decree?

As it voyaged far without a plan,
Finding new spots, there's never a span.
With joy at hand and cheeky mirth,
Who knew a plant could know such worth?

Threads of Life

In corners bright, green leaves entwine,
They twirl and twist like a funky line.
Dance with dust, on shelves so high,
Cheering the sun, as the days pass by.

With every drip, they sip and cheer,
Whispering jokes for the passer's ear.
A blooper reel, in light's warm glow,
They giggle as we tend, oh so slow.

Broad-leafed friends, a silly sight,
Chasing the thrill of the day and night.
In pots and plans, their stories spin,
A comedy show, where life can begin.

Whispering Vines

Vines that laugh and softly tease,
Looping like jump ropes in the breeze.
They chatter tales of a leafy brigade,
Getting tangled in the sunbeam parade.

Each morning's gossip, a cheeky delight,
Chasing dust bunnies in morning light.
With every twist, they playfully splay,
Nature's carnival, come out to play!

Leafy marionettes on display,
Holding a show in a quirky way.
Laughter sprouts where roots embrace,
In whispers of nature, we find our place.

Heartfelt Climb

Climbing high, with a giggle and glee,
Vines scale up with the utmost spree.
Grasping at anything, oh what a game,
A contortionist's dance, just for fame!

They reach for the heavens, on a joyful spree,
Taunting the clouds, as wild as can be.
With every stretch, a new joke spins,
Rooted in laughter, where joy begins.

Nature's comedy, written in green,
With each leafy twist, a funny scene.
A heart full of cheer, as they climb so bold,
Tales of the garden, forever told.

The Soil of Promises

A patch of dirt, where secrets bloom,
Hiding dreams in a cozy room.
Fertilizer mayhem, oh what a show,
With giggles and puns, they steal the glow.

In muddy messes, whims take flight,
Planting hopes under the moonlight.
Every seed, a promise of fun,
Buried deep, till the day is won.

Life's many layers, a comic disguise,
Where laughter sprouts, and joy never dies.
Digging in dirt, with pots piled high,
Sowing our dreams 'neath the big blue sky.

Shades of Resilience

In a corner, green and spry,
A plant reaches for the sky.
Twisting, turning, what a sight,
Chasing sun with all its might.

It resets each time it falls,
No worries, no care at all.
"I meant to do that!" it sings,
Flexing leaves like super springs.

Each vine, a quirky little leap,
Dancing wildly, roots so deep.
Magical mishaps make it glow,
Who knew plants could steal the show?

In chaos, it finds its groove,
Swaying like it's in a move.
With whimsical charm, it defies,
A green comedian in disguise!

Leaves of Abundance

Every leaf a tale to tell,
Absurd secrets do they dwell.
One's stuck in a cat's soft paw,
The others laughing, what a flaw!

Bouncing back from awkward days,
The leaves have quirky, fun ways.
"More sun! Less worry!" they shout,
As squirrels run in circles about.

Green thumbs giggle, prance, and twirl,
In this topsy-turvy world.
With each new shoot, a joke takes flight,
A punchline wrapped in shades of bright.

When storms arrive, they hold a feast,
Puddles splash—oh what a beast!
Nature's party, come and see,
These leaves laugh like they're carefree!

Growing Through Shadows

In twilight's glow, a plant appears,
Whispers jokes to passing dears.
"Why so gloomy, skies above?"
It chuckles, still in love.

Dancing close to shadow's edge,
Cautiously, it makes its pledge.
"Fear not the dark, it's simply fun!"
To gloomy thoughts, it gives a run.

With roots that tickle ground so low,
It knows the secrets shadows show.
"Why wait for sun's warm embrace?"
It teases light with a wild chase.

In every bend, it finds a laugh,
Flipping gloom like a comic's craft.
Growth in shadows? A wild art,
Returning light, a plant's sweet heart!

Nature's Inevitable Dance

Waltzing leaves in gentle breeze,
Nature calls with playful tease.
Roots tap-dancing on the ground,
In a whirl, they're laughing loud!

Flowers twirl with perfect flair,
Bees buzzing, filling up the air.
Each branch swinging, a jolly show,
What a dance, what a flow!

Even rocks have rhythm too,
With moss clapping just for you.
The stars wink in harmony,
As branches sway, a sight to see.

Join the revelry, don't delay,
With nature, there's always play.
In every turn, life's odd trance,
Let's all join this silly dance!

Hidden Treasures in the Leaf

In each green heart, a secret hides,
Where water drips and sunlight bides.
A tiny gnome might just appear,
Holding a thimble full of cheer.

The vines they twist, a merry dance,
Each curl a hint, a fleeting chance.
To find the gold in every turn,
And laugh at leaves that twist and churn.

Just water me and play the tune,
I promise growth by the light of noon.
But step away, don't hold me tight,
I might just sprout wings and take flight!

So gaze upon my leafy prance,
Find joy in the leafy romance.
Each little leaf a quirky jest,
In the garden, I'm truly blessed.

Unwavering Clarity

With every sip, a wink of light,
I reach for sunshine with all my might.
But don't be fooled, I'm still a tease,
I take my time with perfect ease.

In shadows deep, I still do glow,
With clarity that steals the show.
A sneak peek here, a cheeky grin,
Revealing truths that lie within.

So feel my leaves, they're fair and bright,
But watch your step, I might just bite!
With every twist, I try for fun,
In this leafy world, we all are one.

Though I'm a plant, I hold a clue,
To silliness in all we do.
Let laughter sprout and brightly beam,
In every corner, let joy gleam!

Ties that Ground Us

Beneath the soil, my roots they play,
In tangled knots, we laugh all day.
Each wiggly line, a friend so dear,
Join us for fun, we've got good cheer!

We reach for light, but cherish the earth,
In laughter's soil, we find our worth.
With silly games and playful boughs,
We celebrate life, oh, here and now!

Connected through laughter, every inch,
Though dirt might gather, we never flinch.
Hold on tight, but let us sway,
With joy and giggles along the way.

For every fumble, we gleefully bounce,
In our tangled vines, we'll always trounce.
Together we stand, a merry bunch,
In this green world, we'll share our lunch!

Living Testaments of Time

With every leaf, a story spun,
Of sunny days and rainy fun.
A sprinkle here, a sip of rain,
We dance through time, forget the strain.

From tiny sprouts to tendrils long,
We cheer and sing our joyful song.
A twist of fate, a bend of grace,
We relish each leaf, each fun-filled space.

So gather round, and hear us laugh,
As nature scribbles each epitaph.
In every shade, a wink appears,
With tales that bubble and bring good cheer.

So raise a cup to the leaf's grand mime,
A living proof of our fun through time.
With roots and vines, we'll ever climb,
In every moment, pure joy, sublime!

A Promise of Renewal

In the corner, a pot of green,
It's more lively than it could have been,
With leaves that twist and climb so high,
It's the sly plant that'll never die.

Water it once, and it will cheer,
That playful sprite, no need for fear,
In sunlight's glow, it does a dance,
A leafy twirl, oh what a chance!

From stems unbending, roots hold fast,
Its secret shelter from the past,
Grow slowly here, don't rush the day,
This verdant joy, come what may.

Every leaf a little grin,
A plant-like face, cheeky within,
So here's to greens, a grand charade,
In this green world, we've all been played!

Spirals of Tenderness

Spiraling joy, a twisty sight,
Each leaf a laugh, pure delight,
With stems that hug and reach around,
A tender joke that knows no bound.

In shades of emerald, a leafy bloom,
Cleverly hiding from the gloom,
It winks at us from shelf and ledge,
A softy buzzing charming pledge.

This playful prankster on display,
Turns every frown into a fray,
So let's embrace the greenish cheer,
With whispers that are oh-so-clear.

Foliage friends in joyful play,
They'll dance with sunlight every day,
A merry promise in the breeze,
To fill our lives with giggles, please!

Green Gifts of Resilience

A sprightly sprout in a clumsy pot,
Its stubbornness, well, hits the spot,
In every nook, it finds a role,
A jester green, it plays its goal.

Against the odds, it loves to tease,
With dangling leaves that sway with ease,
Who knew a plant could hold such sway,
In its leafy antics, all's okay.

With roots that dig and stretch and grow,
It laughs at storms, puts on a show,
So here's a gift that brings a grin,
A quirky green, we'll let it win!

In every corner, we find our cheer,
A family plant that gathers near,
Its resilience, a story bright,
With leaves of laughter, pure delight.

Echoes of Nature's Embrace

A gentle echo from verdant space,
With quirky curls in fine embrace,
It speaks in growing, leafy tones,
  A playful banter, never alone.

With every twist, a chuckle shared,
Its shrugs and wiggles show it cared,
  In sunny spots, it joins the game,
Building joy, never quite the same.

  A puzzling plant, a silly joke,
  In every droplet, laughter soaks,
So look for smiles in greens around,
Where happiness in leaves is found.

In nature's cradle, fun can thrive,
Around this plant, we come alive,
  An echo of joy, a leafy friend,
In its green giggles, we transcend.

Nature's Gentle Uprising

In the garden where fronds play,
Plants conspire in a leafy ballet.
Vines twist and shout, what a scene,
Whispering secrets of green cuisine.

The squirrels plot with mischief in mind,
While bees dance with a rhythm unrefined.
A cactus wearing shades, oh what flair!
Competing with blooms in the sunlit air.

Rabbits plot their next daring heist,
Nibbling leaves, oh how they feast with pride;
Nature laughs, a quirky jest,
Flora and fauna in a merry fest!

What's this? A mushroom dons a hat,
Inviting friends for a quirky chat.
In this world, strange and sublime,
Nature's laughter echoes through time.

Harmonies of Hope

In the woods where giggles grow,
Saplings strum on strings below.
Ferns clap hands in leafy tones,
Mossy ground beneath their bones.

A neighbor bird with a tune so bright,
Sings to the moon, a silly sight.
Worms wear hats, it's quite a sight,
Jiving to the frogs' delight.

Clouds in the sky play peek-a-boo,
Tickling trees, a playful crew.
Sunflowers sway with giddy grace,
Joining in to this nature race!

The brook chuckles as it flows,
Telling tales of a rose that glows.
Each ripple brings a smile anew,
From nature's heart, a funny cue.

Life's Sustaining Climb

In the backyard, a lizard's flex,
Showcases moves, you'll be perplexed.
A worm is lifting weights, oh dear,
Silly sights bring smiles and cheer.

Climbing high, the ivy grins,
Tickling stones with playful spins.
Its reach is true, yet slippery too,
A comedian in green, it's true!

Amidst the bushes, laughter swells,
With every rustle, a tale it tells.
The sun beams down, a bright-eyed friend,
With winks and nods, the fun won't end!

Turtles race, or so they claim,
In this slowpoke, whimsical game.
Nature's joys, so simple yet grand,
Life's funny climb across the land!

Vines of Expectation

In a pot so small, it dreams of the sky,
A plant on a mission, oh my, oh my!
With a twist and a turn, it stretches with glee,
Its leaves all a-chatter, oh look, look at me!

Neighbors are laughing, they see the plight,
This little green trophy, a heart full of light.
Yet top shelf's too high, the growth won't relent,
A vine of wild schemes that a fence must prevent.

Whispered Green Dreams

Each leaf holds a secret, a giggle or two,
As they jabber softly, 'What else shall we do?'
They plot and they plan like a leafy cabal,
To stretch and to climb, they're having a ball!

With a twist and a reach, they tickle the wall,
While the window frame groans, 'Oh no, not at all!'
Yet in every green whisper and each tiny vine,
Lies an awesome adventure that's shockingly fine.

Tendrils of Hope

Little green fingers, they point to the sun,
In a game of hide-and-seek, they think it's great fun!
Clinging to shadows, they stretch and they sway,
While plotting to overtake the room in a day!

But alas, dear friend, it's a bit of a stretch,
As they cling to the curtains without an etch.
In a tangle of laughter, they never quite land,
Entwined in ambitions just slightly unplanned.

Embrace of the Climbing Heart

With each twist and curl, they dance up so high,
In a comedy show under wide-open sky.
They hug every railing, they wave and they smile,
While causing some ruckus, it's worth every mile!

Through the bemused gaze of the watching pet cat,
The vines toss their leaves like they're home on a mat.
In this climb up the wall, with each tangled part,
Lies a charming embrace of a climbing heart.

Leaves of Lifetime

In corners where the shadow plays,
Green fingers stretch in leafy ways.
They twist and turn, a clever dance,
Poking fun at chance and glance.

A wagging leaf with gentle flair,
Declares to all, 'There's room to spare!'
A little vine that tries to climb,
Whispers jokes in leafy rhyme.

Each twist a giggle, each turn a cheer,
One more layer, 'Can I come near?'
In laughter, roots grow deep and wide,
In pots of dreams, we'll all abide.

Serenity in Spirals

Winding up in spiral style,
Each twist and turn brings a smile.
The leaves are giddy, what a sight!
'Isn't this just pure delight?'

A dance of greens, a leaf parade,
They snorkel in the sunshine shade.
With every spiral, tales unfold,
Of antics from the pot, so bold.

Whispers from the rooted bed,
Tell stories that can't be misread.
With laughter bubbling close at hand,
In leafy joy, together we stand.

Embrace of the Indoor Breeze

A playful gust, it sweeps through here,
Inviting leaves to bounce and cheer.
They wiggle, giggle, dance with flair,
Calling everyone to stop and stare.

Breezes tickle, a plant parade,
Inside the house, no plans to fade.
Each leaf bewitched by airy tunes,
Swinging to the rhythm of afternoon moons.

In potted bliss, they flit and glide,
With every puff, they swell with pride.
The indoor breeze, a merry prank,
In every nook, the leaves, they rank.

A Climbing Dream

In search of heights, they reach and sway,
Peeking out to greet the day.
With hopes as high as any vine,
They dream of scaling, feeling fine.

A leafy crew in wild ascent,
Pushing limits, making rent.
They jibe at pots that hold them back,
In every crack, they plan their track.

With every inch, a story grows,
In curious twists, the laughter flows.
A climbing dream, however tall,
Brings out the charm in one and all.

The Heart of a Climber

A vine I am, with dreams that soar,
I'll reach the ceiling, then ask for more.
In pots I plot my leafy flight,
Expecting sunshine, I'll bask in light.

But who needs dirt? I'll climb the wall,
With pots and hearts, I'll never fall.
A leafy lasso, I twist and twirl,
In the jungle of indoors, I'm queen of the world.

With every twist, a chuckle comes,
I tangle with cables, get stuck on drums.
I promise you leaves, I promise you green,
Let's just not mention how hard I've been seen!

So raise your glasses, make a toast,
To the climbing plant that we love the most.
In laughter we thrive, in sunlight we beam,
A curious climber living the dream.

Flourishing in the Shade

In shadows deep, I find my bliss,
Cleverly dodging the sun's warm kiss.
With a grin, I spread my leaves so wide,
To laugh with the dust bunnies, I take pride.

Though sunbathers preen in their sunny spots,
I sip the cool air while they burn in knots.
My heart is light, my foliage bright,
Shade is my runway, let's take flight!

I'll stretch my vines like I own the place,
While sunflowers bleach in their golden race.
With a wink and a nod to the rays up above,
I thrive in my holler, it's cozy with love!

So here's to the shady, the meek and the mild,
With a sneaky smile, I'm nature's wild child.
In laughter, we flourish, in whispers we play,
Let the sun-birds sing, I'll enjoy my stay.

Nature's Gentle Embrace

In every leaf, a giggle hides,
Nature's touch, where humor abides.
With winds that tickle, and rains that tease,
I dance in the droplets, oh what a breeze!

The moon's a jester in the starlit show,
While clouds do cartwheels, oh how they flow!
Nature's a comedian, can't you see?
With tricks up its sleeve, it's all about glee.

I'll sway with the trees in a playful tune,
While critters around me chaotically croon.
In laughter we blossom, in silliness sprout,
Embracing the quirks that life's all about!

So let's twirl in wildflower fields of delight,
With every little whim, we'll dance through the night.
In nature's embrace, let joy take its stance,
For laughter is life and we've all got a chance!

Loops of Joy

Round and round, I twist and spin,
With laughter echoing, let the fun begin!
In each loop, a story awaits,
Of bumbles and tumbles, and sneaky mates.

I stretch to the ceiling, I weave through the air,
Daring the curtains with joy and flair.
With a wink and a nod, I loop my refrain,
Life's a fun ride, let's dance in the rain!

Like a rollercoaster, up high and down low,
In every fresh twist, hilarity flows.
Life wraps its arms, it spins just right,
In a carnival of colors, oh what a sight!

So come join the loops, let's laugh till we cry,
In this garden of joy, just you and I.
With roots in the ground and dreams in the sky,
Together we'll flourish, together we'll fly!

Verdant Aspirations

In a pot so snug and tight,
Leaves stretch out to greet the light.
I water hope with coffee grounds,
Yet it smiles, the joy abounds.

With each new leaf, I take a chance,
Do they play a leafy dance?
I whisper dreams, they soak it up,
It's like they're sipping from a cup.

A rogue vine takes a daring leap,
Climbs my curtains, oh so steep!
I laugh and watch, can't stop the cheer,
My green pals thrive, that's crystal clear.

So here's to plants, my jolly crew,
With leafy jokes and antics too.
In their green gaze, I find my bliss,
Who knew growth could come with this?

Climbing Towards Tomorrow

A tendril reaches for the skies,
Tickling clouds, oh what a prize!
I can't help but crack a grin,
As my plant dreams to wear a fin.

It trips and stumbles, quite the show,
Who knew plants had such a flow?
I cheer it on, "You got this, mate!"
Shouting bravely, 'Don't let fate wait!'

With each small sprout, I find delight,
New leaves whisper, "We'll take flight!"
It's like a comedy in green,
Nature's humor, truly seen.

So let them climb, let them sway,
In this garden, we all play.
With silly tales in every pot,
Plant humor is what I've got.

Hope Wrapped in Green

In a bright pot, filled with cheer,
I hear my plant shout, "I'm here!"
Leaves like smiles, so fresh and bold,
They dance around in shades of gold.

With pet names like 'Greeny McVine,'
They twist and twirl, feeling fine.
I promise sun and laughter too,
What else can this fine foliage do?

I tell them jokes, they respond in kind,
With every sprout, new laughter we find.
Who knew tangled plants could amuse,
Plant-parent life, I'd never refuse!

So let's celebrate, let's grow in glee,
Nature's comedy, just wait and see!
With every twist, a punchline grows,
Together we'll topple all our woes.

In the Grip of Growth

In my office, a vine takes hold,
Whispering secrets, crazy and bold.
It wraps around my coffee cup,
As if to say, "Don't give up!"

Wobbly legs, a leafy quest,
Each morning brings a new jest.
I marvel at its daring flair,
It's on a mission, unaware!

With hugs of sunshine, warmth, and fun,
What else but joy can be spun?
Each curl and twist, a quirky rhyme,
Growing tales that defy time.

So let's embrace this leafy spree,
In a world of wild greenery.
With every giggle, roots entwine,
My plants and I shall always shine!

Resilient Roots

In a pot that's way too small,
A plant still stands so tall.
With leaves as green as grass,
It laughs at each new task.

Water spilled and soil's mess,
This plant just loves the stress.
With roots that twine and twist,
It reigns, it can't be missed!

Sunlight's sass, a dance of shade,
Each leaf a joke, a leafy blade.
With every droop, it strikes a pose,
A drama queen in chlorophyll clothes.

Chasing light, it makes a fuss,
Yet thrives in shades, not making a fuss.
With a wink and a growing cheer,
This little fella has no fear!

Lush Echoes of Existence

In corners where dust bunnies roam,
A vine drapes down, it calls it home.
Whispering tales of faraway lands,
With each new leaf, it makes new plans.

Its trailing thoughts, a playful tease,
Inviting friends on a leafy breeze.
It giggles softly, sways with glee,
A green comedian, wild and free.

Photosynthesis, a leafy game,
Sipping sunlight, never the same.
With laughter, it drinks from the day,
Sunkissed humor in the display.

Each branch a pun, each leaf a jest,
In this lush life, it's all a fest.
So join the cheer, don't walk away,
In the green theatre, we love to play!

Growth in Stillness

In silence, a sprout cracks the ground,
Not a sound, but joy's profound.
With roots that dig and stretch so wide,
It rivals clouds in the bumpy ride.

Days drift by, the sun's sweet glow,
While this plant shuffles, slow and slow.
Sipping water like a tea so fine,
In the calm, it draws the vine.

No rush, no race, it finds its groove,
In stillness, it learns how to move.
A giggle here, a wiggle there,
Growing tall without a care.

It waves goodbye to speedy plants,
Flaunting those lush leafy pants.
With a chuckle, it takes its time,
In life's slow dance, it's so sublime!

Nature's Everlasting Embrace

In the garden's warm embrace,
Plants wiggle with quirky grace.
A bramble here, a flower there,
Laughing all without a care.

Each petal flirts in the breeze,
Nature's sticky, funny tease.
With roots entwined in merriment,
A chatty bunch of good intent.

From twigs and leaves, a gossip brews,
Silly tales of morning dues.
A salute to raindrops, a wink to the sun,
In this wild realm, we all have fun!

Winds whisper secrets through the trees,
As plants join in with laughter and ease.
In nature's hug, we find our place,
In endless joy, we all embrace!

Threads of Earthly Grace

In the garden, weeds hold dance,
A squirrel sneezes, what a chance!
Roots gossip in the soil's embrace,
While flowers chuckle, full of grace.

Bumblebees wear tiny hats,
Twirling to the sound of chats.
Each petal winks, no need for fuss,
As Mother Nature rides the bus.

Tomatoes blush in bright sunlight,
As frogs croak jokes both day and night.
The sun spills laughter on sweet vines,
Watering hope in silly lines.

Together we laugh, find joy in dirt,
With every new sprout, we flirt.
Nature's humor, wild and free,
Threads of life in harmony.

From Soil to Soul

In the dirt, we plant our dreams,
With a wiggle and some quirky schemes.
Worms wear glasses, reading the ground,
While daisies twirl and spin around.

Roots secretly whisper sweet lies,
As rain showers down, a surprise!
Little sprouts tell secrets too,
Giggling softly, as morning dew.

A carrot blushes, so shy and round,
Hiding under where it's safe and sound.
With each sunrise, a chuckle we share,
Finding warmth in the breezy air.

From soil to soul, a playful leap,
Where joy in growth is ours to keep.
Nature's joke, a delightful spree,
Planting giggles, wild and free.

The Language of Leaves

Whispers flutter through the trees,
As leaves tell tales in the gentle breeze.
One leaf joked, 'I'm not a fan!'
The other sighed, 'Don't be a ran!'

Branches laugh when storms collide,
Creating chaos, a funny ride.
Squirrels chatter, a comic play,
Exposing secrets of the day.

The vines entwine in a playful spin,
Sharing stories of where they've been.
Laughter sprouts in every bough,
Nature's comedy, take a bow!

In the forest, joy is found,
With giggles growing from the ground.
A leafy chorus, sing along,
The language of leaves, a funny song.

Intertwined Futures

In tangled roots, our journeys meet,
Dancing shadows on our feet.
Crickets crack jokes as night draws near,
While moonbeams giggle without fear.

Plants play peek-a-boo with the sun,
Catching rays and having fun.
Beans climb high, waving goodbye,
To the weary earth and painted sky.

Fungi host parties underground,
With mushrooms tapping to a sound.
Upbeat vibes in the loamy glee,
Creating futures, wild and free.

Together we're an earthy choir,
With each sprout fueled by desire.
In harmony, we grow and sway,
Intertwined futures, come what may.

Secrets Among the Shadows

In corners where the green things hide,
Lurks a tale that plants abide.
With tendrils curling, sly and spry,
They giggle softly, oh my, oh my!

Each leaf a whisper, a silent jest,
With soil-mates sharing their leafy quest.
If you peek close, you might just hear,
The laughter growing year by year.

Roots entwined like secret friends,
Trading anecdotes of leafy bends.
A pot of stories, a comedy show,
In the dark, where no one goes!

So if you wander where shadows creep,
Join the laughter, it's quite the leap!
Discover giggles in green galore,
And plant a smile forevermore!

Unexpected Growth

Once a sprout, so small and meek,
Now a vine that's lost its cheek.
It stretches tall and twists around,
In search of sunlight on the ground!

Neighbors look with eyes so wide,
Is that a plant or a green-slide?
It's making friends with all it sees,
And tickling leaves to make them sneeze!

A dance of vines, a wiggle spree,
Who knew green could be so free?
Scaling walls like it's a game,
No rules apply, just viney fame!

From a timid start to bold and brave,
Fueled by giggles, it learns to rave.
With every leaf, a story grows,
Unexpected in the way it flows!

Feeling the Climb

Upward bound, the green things race,
With vines aplenty in the chase.
They scale the shelves, a wild spree,
A leafy ladder, can't climb for free!

Bouncing up with quirky flair,
They poke their heads 'round everywhere.
While humans watch in sheer surprise,
As plants attempt their noble rise!

They swing and sway with giddy cheer,
Join the chaos, have no fear!
For every twist and silly turn,
Is just a lesson that they learn!

So grab a pot and set it loose,
Let greens ascend with razzmatazz juice!
In the climb, there's joy to find,
At the top, it's just unwined!

Sunlight's Embrace

Awake, awake, the sun does call,
Waking green things, one and all.
They stretch and yawn, a brightened scene,
In love with light, a leafy dream!

Oh, how they dance and prance around,
Basking in warmth, they twirl unbound.
With every ray, a giggle grows,
A party's on, as sunlight flows!

They sway their fronds like arms in cheer,
A leafy celebration here!
In sunlight's hug, they feel alive,
With mossy smiles, they thrive and dive!

So let the light pour in anew,
A glow that's bright, a vibrant brew.
In every leaf, a sunny spark,
In the garden's heart, they leave their mark!

The Language of Leaves

In the garden where laughter grows,
Whispers of green in the softest throes.
Leaves chuckle as the sun peeks through,
Speaking secrets that only they knew.

A wobbly vine, with a wiggle and sway,
Tells the tale of a sunny day.
With every curl, a joke it weaves,
Tickling the breeze, as nature breathes.

They gossip in shadows, under the moon,
Chortling leaves, a joyful tune.
Nature's own jesters, in shades of jade,
Mischief unfolds in the leafy parade.

So listen close when the wind takes flight,
For the leaves have stories that shine so bright.
In the language of laughter, they bloom and spin,
Inviting us all to join in the grin.

Journey of a Wayward Vine

A vine with a dream, oh what a sight,
Meandering paths, chasing the light.
With a twirl and twist, it dances along,
Every turn a new laugh, in a playful song.

It swings past the fence with a cheeky grin,
Deciding the world is a place to begin.
Climbing up bricks, it pauses to jest,
"Who needs a plan? I'm just here for the fest!"

Through gardens and gutters, on whimsical rides,
It follows the sun, no worries or guides.
A journey of giggles, this happy green sprout,
With friends in the soil and laughter to tout.

At last, it finds home—a trellis so fine,
A thrilling safe haven for this roguish vine.
It curls up with pride, a triumphant cheer,
For every twist taken brought joy to its sphere.

Spirals of Faith

A leaf takes a leap with a wink and a whirl,
Spinning in circles, giving joy a twirl.
Each spiral a promise, a giggle in bloom,
Dancing through shadows, dispelling the gloom.

In the sunlight's embrace, it finds its way,
Chasing the giggles of a bright summer day.
Roots in the ground, but dreams in the air,
Believing in magic, without a care.

Round and around, the vines play their game,
With every twist, they stake their claim.
In spirals of faith, they frolic and prance,
Eager to join in the swirling dance.

A banquet of laughter, in each leafy curl,
They tease the wind, watch their dreams unfurl.
With sprigs of humor, they sprout and they soar,
In the garden of joy, forever wanting more.

A Tapestry of Verdure

In the fabric of green, threads of delight,
Each stitch a chuckle, each patch a light.
A canvas of joy, with a splash of cheer,
Where leaves gather round, holding stories dear.

Much to their fun, they craft a new scene,
Stitching together the laughter unseen.
Vines twine in harmony, all snug and tight,
Weaving a tapestry, shimmering bright.

With blossoms like jokes, bursting with glee,
Nature's own giggles, as wild as can be.
In hues of verdancy, they paint the space,
A gallery of whimsy, in nature's embrace.

So come take a stroll, beneath this lush scheme,
Where the green leaves conspire, and laughter's the theme.

In the tapestry woven with joy all around,
There's something for everyone—magic is found.

Encounters with the Wild Green

In a corner of my room, it sprawls,
Sneaking peeks at the walls' close calls.
With a twist and a turn, it climbs with great flair,
I leave it alone, it clearly doesn't care.

Each leaf a comedian, rolling its eyes,
While I try to make sense of its leafy lies.
It dances alone in a sunbeam's embrace,
Laughing at me as I trip on my lace.

I've named it Fernando, so full of sass,
In this jungle of home, it's the king of the class.
It whispers sweet nothings to each passing dust,
While I water it daily, fulfilling my trust.

Yet when guests arrive, it hides away shy,
Pretending it's innocent, oh my, oh my!
With a wink and a curl, it jives to the beat,
In the corner it sits, still—an absolute treat.

Whispers of Green Resilience

There's a plant in my kitchen, a real wild child,
Leafy shenanigans, oh how it's compiled!
With roots that stretch deeper than my wildest dreams,
A cardboard box housing emerald schemes.

It chews on the sunlight, swallows the shade,
Telling tales of glory—oh, the trade!
With every little droplet, it giggles with glee,
Like it's plotting a heist just to ghost me.

When autumn rolls 'round and the breezes get rough,
It stands in defiance, oh that's just tough!
Giggling at frost as it snugly wraps tight,
Befriending the chill, it's quite the delight!

So here's to the green that never gives in,
A leafy comedian with a mischievous grin.
In this tapestry of life, it plays its own role,
A resilient spirit that warms up the soul.

Tendrils of Hope

In my messy little corner, green sprouts arise,
Tendrils reaching out like they want the skies.
With a twist and a turn, they climb up my wall,
Making quite a spectacle, a green curtain call!

They tickle the cat, oh what a surprise,
While I laugh and I watch, my heart starts to rise.
Each little green tendril a sprightly performer,
A leafy magician, always the charmer.

I whisper my secrets; it listens so keen,
With leaves that nod gently, oh what a scene!
As it twirls in the sun, it captures the light,
A funny little dance, my day feels just right.

So here's to the joy that it brings on each day,
A bouquet of giggles in its own little way.
With nature as my sidekick, we thrive and we grow,
In this wild and wacky green, love's seeds we sow.

Shadows in the Sunlight

In the corner where sunlight refuses to fade,
A vine weaves stories, with no need for aid.
It tumbles and tumbles, a curious sight,
Casting shadows that giggle, oh what pure delight!

With each leaf that rustles, it shares a small joke,
As I sit here and ponder, sipping on Coke.
Twisting its greens like a master magician,
Oh, the fun of it all, defying tradition!

When the sun spills laughter through leaves of bright green,
It springs into motion, the life of the scene.
An entertainer bold, with tendrils so spry,
Chasing away dullness as the moments slip by.

So here's to the shadows, where silliness rules,
A plant with a sense of humor, so cool!
In this room of quiet, it adds vibrant cheer,
With whispers of joy that I hold oh so dear.

Dreams in a Sunlit Corner

In a corner, dreams do sprout,
Chasing sunlight, there's no doubt.
Leaves unfurl with such great cheer,
Whispering secrets only we hear.

With each sip of morning dew,
They laugh and dance, oh what a view!
A twist, a curl, a bit of fun,
Who knew green could chase the sun?

Potted friends in joyful glee,
Making puns with bumblebees.
Cracks in pots, a graceful mess,
Chortling blooms in their own dress.

Oh, the tales these leaves could tell,
With laughter ringing like a bell.
In sunlit corners, life's pure joy,
A leafy romp, a playful ploy.

Nurtured by Light

In the glow where shadows play,
Leaves hold court and gently sway.
Sunbeam hugs, they stretch and pose,
Fashionable greens in funny clothes.

A mischievous vine wraps so tight,
Twirling fellow neighbors just right.
A tickle here, a wiggle there,
Who knew plants could have such flair?

They bask in rays, a warm embrace,
With every sip, they pick up pace.
Craving laughter, they sprout and scheme,
A leafy world, a shared dream.

Lighthearted whispers fill the air,
In this garden, love's declared.
Swaying softly, they delight,
Nurtured boldly by the light.

Echoes of Nature's Whisper

In the breeze, a secret's sung,
Tales of tittering leaves so young.
Vines entwined, they sway and wink,
A leafy jest that makes us think.

Moths pirouette, all dressed in night,
While crickets play a tune so bright.
Nature giggles in soft tones,
Rooted joys, no need for phones.

Wandering bees buzz a refrain,
Mixing hues of yellow and grain.
With every petal, laughter spreads,
A chorus sung on leafy beds.

Life's a jest, wrapped in green rhyme,
Tickling softly, transcending time.
Echoes hum and rustle true,
In this garden, all colors renew.

The Heart's Green Embrace

Amongst the tendrils, love does twine,
A heart that beats with leaves divine.
In playful jests they intertwine,
Green giggles lighten every line.

Fronds on frolic, reaching high,
As if to touch the bluest sky.
In each curl, a winking jest,
What's life without a little zest?

Plants plotting mischief in the shade,
Inverdant whims, not a moment's made.
Bumbling bees, a joyful throng,
Celebrating life, singing their song.

With every leaf, a chuckle shared,
An embrace where nothing's spared.
Silly hearts of green, so bold,
A comic tale of life retold.

Nature's Commitment

In a pot with plenty of space,
A green vine decided to race.
With a little twist and turn,
It vowed to steal the spotlight and earn.

With leaves like smiles, it waved at the sun,
Saying, 'Watch me, I'm second to none!'
Roots tangled up like a game of charades,
Nature giggled, 'Oh, look at these escapades!'

A spider stopped by, gave a nod,
'You're growing well, without a façade!'
The vine just shrugged, doing its thing,
In a jungle of pots, it was the king.

But with every twist, it bumped on a shelf,
'Just minding my business,' it said to itself.
Leaves laughed softly, whispering low,
'Let's see how far this can go!'

The Patience of Growth

In silence, a sprout made its claim,
Holding on tight, it played the waiting game.
Days turned to weeks, roots growing slow,
'Why can't I hurry?' it whispered below.

Sunlight tickled its tender green face,
'You're not a rocket, this isn't a race!'
Each morning it stretched, looking for cheer,
While a snail passed by, whispering, 'Dear!'

Seasons changed, yet the sprout held its ground,
With a wink and a giggle, it twirled around.
'There's no rush,' it hummed with delight,
As it plotted in dreams to reach for new heights.

When at last it became a grand vine,
With tangled leaves, looking mighty fine.
A lesson learned in each little sprout,
Delay can lead to fun without doubt!

Climbing Towards Tomorrow

In the corner, a green climber sighed,
'No ladder, but I'll rise with pride.'
With a wink to the wall, it made its appeal,
'Let's have a race, I'll show you zeal!'

A paint can chuckled back from the ground,
'You won't get far, my friend, look around!'
But up it went, with leaves all aglow,
Imagining heights and new places to grow.

'Just a little more,' the climber would say,
As it reached for the edge, not wanting to sway.
'Gravity, please, let me just have fun,
There's a view at the top, I've got to run!'

Finally, it touched the ceiling's height,
'Guess who's above? I'm taking flight!'
The room cheered on, hearts filled with glee,
'Climb on, little friend, you're wild and free!'

Leaves in the Wind

Little leaves danced in the breeze,
Spinning around, full of such ease.
'This is our stage,' they gleefully chimed,
While the branches just swayed in sublime.

One leaf said, 'Look, I'm a helicopter!'
While another spun, feeling quite proper.
'Catch me if you can!' they giggled and twirled,
As they floated down from their leafy world.

A gust came by, they all held on tight,
'Whoa, there's no way we're giving up the fight!'
With a daring flip, they let out a roar,
'The sky is our dance floor, let's ask for more!'

As the sun set low, and colors turned bright,
Leaves whispered secrets in the fading light.
'Let's promise to sway and laugh till the end,
A waltz in the wind, my leafly friend!'

Seasons of Renewal

When winter whispers, leaves turn shy,
They huddle close, like friends gone dry.
But spring arrives, with laughter and glee,
Green friends emerge, as bright as can be.

Oh summer's sun, you bring the cheer,
Climbing high, we sip our beer.
With every breeze, a little dance,
Nature's joke, a leafy prance.

Then autumn comes, time to shed,
Colors burst, a feast instead.
While squirrels scamper, round they scurry,
In this mad world, no time to worry.

Through every season, life has a tease,
Pothos laughing in that gentle breeze.
We'll keep climbing, it's quite the race,
Because who knows, we might win first place!

An Ode to Climbing Journeys

Oh tiny vine, with dreams so tall,
You wrap your way around it all.
With every twist and cheeky smile,
You make us laugh, climb every mile.

In the corner, there's a shelf,
You think you'll climb above yourself?
But oops! A cat dashes past,
Your leafy game, not built to last.

Through pots and books, you find your way,
Dodging dust as if to say—
"I'll conquer heights, I'll show my friends,
That little old me can reach the ends!"

So here's to you, dear climbing mate,
With every vine, you navigate.
Keep cracking jokes in your bright green hue,
The world's a jungle, thanks to you!

Harmony in the Canopy

Up in the leaves, a party's set,
In the canopy, we'll never fret.
Singing birds and monkeys swing,
It's a wild world that makes us grin.

Green pals gossip, sunbeams play,
Photosynthetic dance all day.
From one branch to another, they cheer,
As vines embrace without any fear.

The wise old tree tells tales anew,
Of childhood dreams, of wanting to brew.
But lightning struck, oh what a plight,
Now everyone's buzzing, 'Hold on tight!'

So let's climb high, don't miss the fun,
In the canopy, we've all just begun.
With laughter echoing through the space,
Join the dance, it's a leafy race!

The Art of Tenacity

Oh stubborn vine, with roots so bold,
You grip the pot, a sight to behold.
Through sunshine, shadows, highs and lows,
You keep on growing, that's how it goes!

For every wilt, you shake it off,
A sprout of hope, you'll never scoff.
You twist and turn, a crafty plea,
Don't underestimate your tenacity!

A watering can, your greatest friend,
With every sip, on growth you depend.
When life gets tough, you'll find a way,
In your leafy heart, a giggle stays.

So here's to you, oh mighty green,
In this jungle, you reign supreme.
With every struggle, watch you exceed,
The art of tenacity, indeed, indeed!

www.ingramcontent.com/pod-product-compliance
Lightning Source LLC
Chambersburg PA
CBHW050305120526
44590CB00016B/2500